Spiralling into Substance

Ayla Fawad

BookLeaf Publishing

India | USA | UK

Presentation by *BookLeaf Publishing*

Web: www.bookleafpub.com

E-mail: info@bookleafpub.com

ISBN: 9789358319026

First edition 2023

Like A Flower

Like a flower
You're made of beautiful stuff
You keep on growing
With your colors gently showing
When your days are grey
and your times are rough
Like a flower's petals
You absorb what's good
The light from the sun
And the warmth of someone
Makes you feel at one
When your soul comes undone
And brings you back as it should
Like a flowers' stem
You hold yourself up
Standing strong and tall
Through the harshest of winds
Through pain
Through it all
And the world will still admire
The beauty of you
Through every rise and every fall

Lost Words

I consciously get back up and sit down
With a beautiful notebook
A pen drooling with ink
A burning desire
A careful plan
To write out my mind
That which has brought me a valuable find
I become wordless
My thoughts are on pause
I can't expurge words on par with me
Those deep conversations
That should be had with paper
Do appear
But at the worst of times
While tossing and turning
Drifting off to sleep
Sometimes I scribble some of those thoughts
But the adequacy is lost to my dreams
To my unconscious
And maybe they're better off there

Blue Romance

I hurt myself again
Thinking you really cared
But you're just so broken
And I am just so scared
Scared to give all of me
To an empty shell
To face the rejection I know so well

I have so much shit to do
And I'm simmering in thoughts of you
Although I know its an excuse
To murder the time I have for something new
Because I love the pain of feeling blue

There

You can fall apart in front of me
I will still be there
To help you pick up the pieces
As much as you can bear
You can shout for the skies to shake
You can scream and swear and ache
And I won't cower away
You can invade my personal space
I'll only step back
But I'll stay
I'll sit with you in your pain
Until it goes away
As long as you shall say
I can sit with you all day

Insomnia

There are parts of me
That I can't be
In this old and forgotten sea
My soul is broken
But my thoughts are free
My brain is swollen and I fail to sleep
There is something there
In the depth of my despair
And in the unsuccessful counting of sheep
But the search is endless
And it feels unfair

Perhaps the universe keeps us awake
intentionally
So we can have a quiet conversation with the
moon
Describing our thoughts and worries relentlessly,
Eloquently
Finding the most unusual solutions
Like poetry

Sunset

A most beautiful part of day
When the darling sun has had it's say
As the moonlights calling
It can no longer stay
Colors of pink, orange, and red fade into grey
And this magnificent occurrence is just part of
nature's way
The rise and fall of the sun
The most beautiful and yet the most fun
When the novelty of a clear plate
Of a new day
Has just begun
When all the things have been said and done
Nothing to do and nowhere to run
We know for certain that nature has won

Scrolling

You are not the entirety of me
Only a fragment
Of my story
And I yours
I am whole
With or without you

Sometimes I seek completion
Of my rotten obsession
But that doesn't mean I'm in love

You're an enigmatic thought
Engraved in my brain

Bedbug to my whatever makes me sane

Recycling

Recycle pens and paper
Anything and everything plastic
Recycle your thoughts but don't be too drastic
Recycle your journey
To ensure you have passed it
Recycle your happiness
As soon as you've amassed it
Recycle your world
So you feel that it has lasted

Us

We all feel broken, beaten, battered
We all feel bruised
We all feel shamed, shaken, shattered
We all feel used
We all are individuals
But we all are also fused

Unedited Love

I want the unedited version of you
I want your scruffy hair
Your morning face
I want to know your terrible thoughts
I want to know every version of you
Your red and blue
I want to feel all your parts
The parts you don't want to know yourself
Of yourself
I want the honest truth
Your thoughts of me
Of us
But what I need is not you
And I don't need thoughts of you
And I don't need to know your thoughts of me
I don't need to want you

Something

We're afraid of nothingness
Becoming nothing
All while we are not nothing
Atleast not nothing yet
We are still something

Spring

Spring is the season that sings
When butterflies and moths alike flaunt their
wings
When the sun shines but the heat stings
Spring is the birth of colors
Of blue, of red, of green, of pink
Of beautiful things
That is the abundance of beginnings that spring
brings

She

She is kindness and passion
She is nurturing and whole
She is the best kind of fashion
She is a beautiful soul

She is a mother
She is a daughter
She is a friend
She was but she still is
She is never going to end

She is mostly strength
She could go to any length
She is the notion that passion prevails
And hard work never fails

Straighten

14

Maybe it's my sudden weakness
It's the universe teaching me a lesson
Maybe I deserve to feel like this
Because I knew it was wrong
Whatever I felt
But I followed that feeling anyway
Out of loneliness or self sabotage
The universe is straightening me out
It knows what's no good for me

Write Right

Write it out
Write it down
Words on paper
In poetry, let's drown
Write out your pain to wash it away
Write out your dreams
So in your heart they will stay
Write out your life
To start fresh everyday

Autumn

When the leaves are falling
You know Autumn's calling
When the sun don't shine
Autumn's standing in line
When the trees have gracefully aged
You know Autumn can't be staged
The goldening of roses
And the sniffling of noses
Gives you insight
To when Summer finally closes

Not Worthy

If you show me you don't care about my feelings
You're not worthy of me
If you actively push me away
You're not worthy of me
If you actively avoid deeper conversations with
me
You're not worthy of me
If you make me feel unwelcome, undesired,
uncomfortable
You're not worthy of me
If you make me question my own worth, how
can you ever be worthy of me?

Stop

Stop staring at me
With those ill intentioned eyes

I'm not your possession
I'm not your prize

I'm not something you can achieve
With just a few tries

I'm a person
I'm a woman
A daughter, a sister
A colleague, a friend

I'm not and will never be
Your means to an end.

Uncomfortable Dialogue

"Will you watch my bag while I get coffee?"
"Yes okay sure."
"Where you going?"
Silence.
"I need to get coffee too."
"Are you married?"
"No."
"Do you want me?"
"No thanks, I have a boyfriend."
"Are you being courted?"
"Sorry I don't understand."
"Do you have a boyfriend?"
"Yes I do."
"How old are you?"
"24"
"Guess how old I am?"
"I'm sorry I'm not sure."
"Just give it a guess."
"60?"
"I'm 73."
"Oh wow."
"Yeah wow."
Looks into my laptop
Netflix 'who's watching'
"Who's watching? Haha"

"It's Netflix where you can watch movies and television."
Sees YouTube, "What's that?"
"You can watch video clips"
Lady approaches and talks to him
"She's just a friend"
 Okay?

Taking Peace

Our parents may never understand what they
did
We may never understand why they did what
they did
We can take peace knowing they tried their best
with what they had
Those that had no ill intent
The tools they were given and the tools that they
found
Some of those tools were broken with sharp
edges
This doesn't take away the impact
Doesn't minimise our pain
Doesn't justify anything
But to learn that it's pain morphed into pain
Softens the perception of it
Scars begin to heal
And we begin to feel able to breathe

Commute

The clouds and metal tracks align
The hesitant sun looking oh so fine
Hiding behind shadows of a forgotten place
Immersed in the cycle of the daily rat race

Gloomy turquoise skies
Monday morning blues
An double espresso in her eyes
For the slumber she did lose

Bodies in greys, greens, blacks and blues
intertwined
Like a game of twister but with an inner desire
to rewind
Back to childhood moments where these stances
felt free
Rather than entrapped in the projection of who
they need to be

Many necks bent downwards in a zombie like
state
The abundance of worlds within worlds in one
place
All in a rush to meet their goals, create their fate

He sees a need and offers his seat, with kindness
and grace